SUSA

A Graceful Goodbye

A NEW OUTLOOK ON DEATH

dp

Copyright

Difference Press

Washington, DC, USA

Copyright © Susan B. Mercer, 2017

Published 2017

ISBN: 978-1-68309-204-9

DISCLAIMER

Cover Design: Michelle Grierson

Editing: Grace Kerina

Cover photograph courtesy of Nicola Holly Louise Mercer

Author's photo courtesy of Dr. Ronald Holt.

DEDICATION

I dedicate this book to all the people who have shared their end-of-life with me, showing me the peace and ease of how death can occur beautifully and gracefully.

Table of Contents

Introduction

As we think about life, we must think about death. As we think about death, we must think about life. Life and death go hand in hand. There is no life *or* death, only life *and* death. Why do we fear death so much then? Is it because we don't *how* we will die? Do we fear life as much?

What does it mean to live, to be alive? The Webster's Dictionary definition of life is "a state of living characterized by capacity for metabolism, growth, reaction to stimuli and reproduction."

Think back to your childhood. Play was involved – lots of play, learning and discovering, being curious, and asking lots of questions, sometimes not even bothering to listen for the answer. When did the questioning, curiosity, and discovery stop, and why?

In our teen years, we may have explored more and expanded and contracted ourselves based on our peers' reflections, and then taken that knowledge into our twenties, when more exploration occurred, through college or jobs.

In all this living, where does death fit in?

Someone you knew may have died (ceasing to live in this dimension) during those years. You didn't forget about them then. Their memory lived on. Was the grief and sorrow unbearable or were you able to move beyond that and celebrate the times you'd had together? Did you change how you lived because of knowing them?

The Webster's Dictionary definition of death is "the irreversible cessation of all vital functions especially as indicated by permanent stoppage of the heart, respiration, and brain activity: the end of life."

It is possible to live well and to die well. Being prepared to live seems automatic. To live well and fully means to live consciously, not zombie-like, to connect with other humans, animals, and nature. We prepare for living by seeking education, jobs, vacations, etc., yet we tend to become like an ostrich in the sand when it comes to death, thinking it won't happen to us.

No one receives a "Get out of death free" card. Imagine how crowded this planet would be if we humans didn't die and nothing else died. There would be no room for co-creation. If nothing died – trees, flowers, birds, fish, insects – where would everything fit? There is only so much room.

The circle of life includes death. Thinking about dying

and death can conjure ideas of pain and struggle. My wish for you is to see it differently. Our bodies are created with an expiration date, though we don't know when that date is. Sure, technology has advanced and increased our days, it's not a given it has increased the quality of our life.

As we think about death and explore its meaning and our fears, we can change our perceptions and find greater connection and ease.

The fear of death is a fear of the unknown. So let's look at death and create some new ideas around it. Let's look at the possibilities of what death is, aside from our preconceived notions, and expand our awareness. Changing a perspective can alter the outlook. Imagine how different we might be if we lived our lives as if we were dying. Because we all are. We might value life differently, then.

This book is about life, living fully, and discovering what that actually means. It is also about death, dying fully, and deciding what that means.

If you've been drawn to this book because a loved one is dying, you'll find solace here, along with practical tools for looking at difficult issues around life and death. We're going to look at being prepared for death by consciously exploring how you feel, how your loved one wants to be remembered, what your loved one wants their experience to be as they are dying, and helping your loved one state their wishes for family and medical staff.

This can strengthen your loved one's eternal flame and help them leave with a graceful goodbye.

CHAPTER 1

Emotions

"When thinking about life remember this: no amount of guilt can solve the past and no amount of anxiety can change the future."

—womenworking.com

Our emotions change so much, yet so much of life stays the same. When we think of death or realize our loved one may be dying sooner than later, all our fears surrounding life and death rise to the surface.

Feeling Grief, Sorrow, and Sadness

Oh no, this can't really be happening. Now what? As you deal with someone who is dying, strong feelings may come over you. You may feel unprepared and wonder how to get prepared, to see and converse with your loved one and the family. A sense of overwhelming grief may rise from the pit of your stomach – and your loved one hasn't even died yet.

It can sometimes seem as if we are treating our dying loved one as if they are already gone, while they are still physically here.

Why is it we tend to tune out before we need to? What is it we don't want to face? Is it our own mortality? You may be thinking, *This is the time I want to be with them the most; yet I'm not sure what to do.* What if they don't realize they are dying – then what? Most people do have an inner sense of knowing they are dying as their end draws near. Most times, they are not sure how to tell their loved one, as they are fearful of leaving that person and are concerned for their loved one's well-being.

Being open and honest with your loved one who is dying can give them a sense of your well-being and while you will miss them, you will be okay. Questions like those above certainly can be difficult questions to ask, especially if *you* haven't thought of them before. Asking and answering some of these questions for yourself gives you a better understanding. And doing so, is also preparation for when you depart this physical world. This may be the catalyst for having your loved one feel they can share their feelings, fear, anxiety, and hopes, and say what they want their death to be like.

Do you think it's death your loved one may be fearing the most, or how they will die?

Coming to terms with your own feelings of death and mortality may ease and create a more open, honest relationship and communication with your parent, sister, brother, spouse – whoever it is who is transitioning. As you acknowledge your fears and sorrow, you allow the other person to express their fears as well. This open dialogue strengthens the communication about death, and may open your heart, too. Anything is possible; and maybe life is eternal even though the physical body has "left." Would facing this ease your pain and suffering? Might it ease the pain and suffering of your loved one?

Many "things" in our lives die. It could be a friendship that ended while the person was still physically here. Divorce is another type of death of a physical, intimate relationship gone and not knowing what is next. The sense of the "unknown" can bring up fear. Every time there is an ending of some sort, it is a type of death, even if we don't choose to see it that way. After you've accomplish a goal you set, do you sometimes experience a let-down instead of feeling glory or relief? That let-down is a death of sorts. What about the loss of a job? Losing a job may feel like a death.

What about weight loss? Maybe the reason we struggle so much with losing weight is because we haven't come to terms with fully embracing what that weight did for us, much less bless it and move on. We mourn the loss of the weight, as other emotions arise we don't want to deal with. The cells of our body die every second as new cells are generated.

The death of a thing or person creates the opportunity to fully understand and be curious about our own mortality.

Take a look at what has died in your life – maybe an old job, moving away from a familiar place, etc. What was your experience of that loss? Did you just turn away, as if it didn't matter, or did you wonder why you were sad for a while afterwards? Looking at the reasons may be a way for you to relate to death with your loved one. Perhaps, ask them about something or someone who has died in their life. Ask them about how they feel/felt. This may be the opening they need to talk with you about death. You can even ask them, "Have you ever thought about your own death?"

We make future plans for vacations, retirement, IRAs, yet we fail to make plans or to make our wishes known around death until we become sick or too old to be able to do so without a lot of help. As Ben Franklin said, "There are two things you can count on in life, Death and Taxes." We pay taxes, but we choose not to prepare for death. Why? I ask myself this question regularly. I am not afraid of death, because I believe we are all eternal spiritual beings having a human experience, yet I, too, have procrastinated in making my end of life wishes known to my loved ones.

What about you? Have you made any plans for your end of life? Perhaps, thinking about this coming to the end of life phase has you worried and anxious.

Religious Connotations

I am not a religious person, yet I find these passages to be helpful in understanding forgiveness:

- "All of us are imperfect." –James 3:2
- "Do unto others as you would have them do unto you." –Luke 6:31

Death has many religious connotations. Be curious about how you really feel about the hereafter. According to the www.dummies.com article, "Taking a Look at Jewish Religious Beliefs," "Judaism was the first tradition to teach *monotheism*, the belief that there's only one God. As Judaism evolved, the idea of God evolved, too, focusing on One unknowable, universal, image-less Being, Who, because the universe is framed in Love, requires justice of human beings." According to www.infoplease.com, "The central teachings of traditional Christianity are that Jesus is the Son of God, the second person of the Trinity of

God the Father, the Son, and the Holy Spirit; that his life on earth, his crucifixion, resurrection, and ascension into heaven are proof of God's love for humanity and God's forgiveness of human sins." Thich Nhat Hanh, a Buddhist monk, shares these thoughts in his book, *No Death, No Fear*: "Birth and death are notions. They are not real. The fact we think they are true makes a powerful illusion that causes our suffering. The Buddha taught that there is no birth; there is no death; there is no coming; there is no going; there is no same; there is no different; there is no permanent self; there is no annihilation. We only think there is. When we understand that we cannot be destroyed, we are liberated from fear. It is a great relief. We can enjoy life and appreciate it in a new way."

Consider a variety of religious and spiritual teachings and examine which best resonates with you. Ask the ill/dying person what resonates the most with them. Knowing your own belief system may open the door for questions and conversation, all the while remembering you have your own viewpoint and there is no right or wrong, good or bad opinion. Be curious as to why your loved one believes what they do, and be prepared to explain why you believe what you do. Thoughts are just thoughts. These conversations may hold the magic for dying perfectly.

Relationships

Facing and exploring how you feel is so important in supporting someone else through this process. If you feel you are not able to have these important conversations about death and dying on your own, you can seek counsel from a pastor or minister from church, a hospice volunteer or nurse, or an End of Life Doula. They may be better able to elicit these conversations and create the pathway for open discussions between you and your loved one.

Sometimes, we may feel we have to die perfectly, just as we often feel we have to live perfectly. But what does that even mean? How does one die perfectly? Perhaps, to die perfectly one needs to let go, to release fears, regrets, and shame.

When we give forgiveness, show gratitude, and have *real, honest conversations*, we encourage the people around us to be fully present, to listen to us and hear us without judgment.

Are you able to have honest communication with your loved one? Have you shown forgiveness and gratitude toward your loved one if they've needed it? Can you imagine what that experience would be like, to feel like to receive someone's forgiveness and gratitude? Take a deep breath and try to imagine. How you want someone to show up for you, may be the key to how you can show up for them. Would you want them to have a painted on smile, or be truthful with their feelings. Maybe you won't like what they have to say. Being present, though, may give you the ability to really hear them from your heart place.

Heart to heart communication begins and renews true connections. Compassion for someone else, especially your loved one, is essential.

Maybe what your loved one has to share is something so profound, and you had no idea your loved one felt that way. Listen openly and honestly, with vulnerability and with no expectation of the outcome. Be peaceful, happy, and grateful you have the opportunity for these conversations. Would you want your loved one to hide their fears of sadness and grief or to be open and vulnerable with you? Just imagine your loved one sitting and being with you, just as they are, and you sitting and being with your loved one just as you are, no false pretenses.

This sharing may give each of you the opportunity and permission to openly show your emotions instead of having to put on a brave facade. And you don't have to fix them or discourage your loved one from crying. You don't have to make everything okay. You can both just *be*, sharing a beautiful, compassionate, heartfelt moment.

So many times, we navigate this life according to what others think, instead of from our own inner guidance. But when you can be truly honest with yourself, you are then able to be honest with the other person. Be honest and have the conversations you need to have. "I really did not like how you treated me when you did that" (whatever it was). Or you may want to say, instead, "I felt hurt how you avoided me at the party five years ago" (it's amazing how long we can hold grudges). Or "I felt ashamed when you slapped me." Being aware of our phrasing can change the statement from one of blame and judgment to one of simply owning our feelings.

The person's response might be, "Oh my goodness, I did not realize you felt that way. I'm so sorry." And, all in a matter of minutes, you've owned your feelings in an honest, un-accusatory way and received an apology. Of course, it won't always happen this way, however, you do have the ability to practice this way of being, which can help to create the types of results leaving you both feeling better.

I've often heard of how a mother doesn't speak to her son or daughter, how a father doesn't speak to his brothers or sisters, because of a past incident. Why? What is so horrible that days, weeks, months, years slip by with no communication? Which is worse, having (what's perceived as) a tough conversation and giving forgiveness, or realizing someone is dying or has already died and you never took the chance to tell them how you really felt?

Personally, I'd rather have the conversation. Having these types of conversations with your loved one may ease the anxiety you are feeling about the death of your loved one, and may help them, too.

I've experienced how much healing can happen when a person says, "I forgive you. Please forgive me. Thank you. I love you."

Recognizing and Coping with Buried Emotions

Our unresolved emotions can hold us back and keep us in that trapped, uncommunicative, seemingly uncaring world. Are you carrying baggage from an incident a while ago? For us to evolve spiritually and emotionally, forgiveness is a key component, even with abusive or violent people – actually, most especially with them. You are not condoning the wrong or acting as if the situation never happened; you are simply letting it go, moving from the past to the present to create a different future.

Forgiving enables you to set an example of generosity and unconditional love. This may also encourage the other person to ask for forgiveness or to apologize.

It is important, when forgiving someone, to not let expectations get in the way. You are forgiving yourself by letting go of whatever may have happened. Studies have been conducted which showed that an abused person forgiving the perpetrator resulted in the abused person feeling more happiness, confidence, and understanding of unconditional love and relationships. Holding on to rage, anger, or shame may increase what we attract to us and hold us prisoner. Letting go gives us freedom.

Forgiveness may be the key to unlocking negative feelings toward someone. Try it. Try forgiving the person you thought you would never speak to again and yet would feel remorse about if you never forgave them while they were alive. Forgiving doesn't mean you will then be best friends or have a relationship. It will bring you ease, peace, and happiness. Try it and see how you feel. You really have nothing to lose.

Exercise: Forgiveness and Gratitude

An exercise for forgiveness, which can be helpful if you are not ready for a personal conversation, is to write a letter to the person you want to forgive. You may or may not send it, but just writing this letter can aid you in seeing the situation differently or it may help you lose some of the meaning and anger you gave to the situation and person. This can assist in neutralizing the hurt.

I find doing this helpful if I decide I want to then have the conversation, as I have something to refer to. Sometimes, just writing the letter can ease the angst you've been feeling.

You can also write a letter to someone who has passed you wish you'd forgiven. Forgive them now.

Forgiveness is also important to give to yourself. Make a list of things you forgive yourself for. As you inhale, ask for forgiveness and, as you exhale, let it go. Acknowledging your feelings in this way, may help relieve some of the stress and anxiety you may be experiencing regarding your loved one's upcoming death.

Gratitude is the other important consideration when working through emotions. Be grateful every day for whatever comes your way. Make a list in the morning as you are waking up, even before you get out of bed, of three things you are grateful for and, if possible, say them aloud and write them down. Every night, just before bed, in the stillness, say and write 3 things you are grateful for. Try to be grateful for 6 different things each day for a week.

How do you feel when you do this?

You can choose a topic and look for things in it to be grateful for, like yourself, other people, nature, or whatever. You may consider making this a daily practice. Topics may be repeated after a week, if necessary. It will be interesting, though, to see how you begin to notice the simpler things in life. It is really easy to notice the big things; noticing the little things on a daily basis makes the most difference.

I practice this gratitude process while lying in bed before falling asleep, and upon waking while I stretch. You can do this over morning coffee. "I am grateful for my strong body that allows me to walk every morning. I am grateful for my invigorating walk to calm my mind this morning as it prepares me for my day." You may also use the morning gratitude to create the gratitude topic for the evening.

This gratitude exercise helps to hold you accountable, yet is not necessary. Try it and see how you feel. Notice in your body where you hold tension and breathe to release it as you imagine the gratitude of you being the ideal you. Once you've practiced this, you can share and encourage your loved one to do the same.

Especially as your loved one's end of life draws near, expressing gratitude for all your loved one has and had may ease their pain and suffering.

You may, at this point, be asking something like, "how can I be grateful for an abusive relationship?" Forgiveness and gratitude help us navigate our inner selves and take responsibility for *our own* actions and responses. We are not responsible for others' actions. We learn our lessons through positive and negative experiences, which keep us on course and allows us to access our inner GPS. But there is always more than one path. No path is more right than the other. Whatever path you choose is the ideal one at this time.

The release and letting go of forgiveness may give you space for a new experience, hopefully a positive one. Gratitude also provides space to create a new adventure. When you hold onto all the old stuff of your past, there is little or no room for something new to emerge. Forgiveness is like cleaning house and getting rid of the clutter. Gratitude is the icing on the cake of how you feel better, once the clutter is released. Sink into these feelings.

As you come to terms with your emotions and show forgiveness and gratitude, you enable the other people (family, friends) to do the same. Imagine a family celebration where no judgments are held, no grudges, no ill will, just unconditional love, laughter, and fun. That's my kind of party.

Now you've created the space to be totally present for your loved one. Show your loved one unconditional love, support, and understanding at the time they need it the most. This support may give your loved one the serenity they need to release into their next phase peacefully.

"Do not dwell in the past,

do not dream of the future,

concentrate the mind on the present moment."

–Buddha

NOTES

CHAPTER 2

Celebration of Life

"The real question is not whether life exists after death. The real question is whether you are alive before death."

—Osho

When we are born, usually there is much celebration: balloons, stuffed animals, cigars, oohs and aahs – showcasing the accomplishment of a life being brought into this world. Then the celebrations happen every year, around your birthday.

What if every day were a celebration of life?

Children embrace each day as if yesterday didn't exist. Some may cry upon waking; however, most open their eyes in wonder at what the new day may hold for them. It may be the discovery of fingers and toes, the flitting of a butterfly outside the window, the sound of a bird chirping. Usually, it is the little things children notice the most.

When was the last time you noticed the butterflies or listened to birds chirping? I think you do care about the little, wonderful things, and yet, maybe you are plodding through your day oblivious to your surroundings, too caught up in what's at hand. The bird doesn't really care if you notice; it will sing anyway. The butterfly will still flit by, whether you see it or not. When you take the time to notice, to observe how another life is living, you have the opportunity to change how you live.

You may find yourself breathing more, really breathing deeply instead of only doing shallow breathing. You may take the time to notice the clouds moving and their formations, the tree's branches bending to the wind with their leaves rustling, and really, really noticing life happening all around you. Sure, there may be traffic; traffic is life happening. Maybe the horns you hear honking are a wake-up call to wake up right here, right now and be present in *this* moment in time. What could be more important? Why do we wait to live, so we can wait to die? Well, that doesn't make much sense, since we fear death. So why wait for it? Death will happen anyway. We just don't know the how or the when.

Why We Are Here

Living fully means living in the *present* moment. Sure, the past has happened, and perhaps many lessons have been learned, so learn from them, and let them go to make space for the next adventure, which is happening now. We are here to sense.

You can create what you want the future to look like; you can't really live in the future. You can only live in the here and now. Be fully present. Notice your surroundings. You've created them, so wake up to them daily without numbness. Use all five senses to observe where you are at any given moment.

See if you can notice without judgment ("That tree should be taller and greener." Why? "That bird's chirping is too loud." Why?). Just stop and notice the beauty of the trees, the sounds of the birds. What do you smell? Just notice. – is the aroma pleasant or stinky? If stinky, you can make a choice to find a more pleasant scent, without attaching a story.

What about taste? You have a sense of taste to determine if something is spicy, bland, hot, cold, pleasing or not – that is how you can discern and learn of your likes and dislikes. Do you pay attention to your sense of taste when eating, savoring every bite, or do you just eat to eat, not caring or wondering where your food came from. Food is life source, giving life and nourishing your body.

Explore your sense of touch, noticing whether something is hot, cold, soft, hard, dry, wet. This helps you discern what you want.

Think about the music you listen to and why. What sounds generate feelings of ease, pep, danger, alertness, excitement or joy?

What aromas do you surround yourself with? Notice which ones give you a sense of calm, which others give you more energy. Lavender and peppermint are examples of scents that usually generate a calm or energized feeling.

What are your preferences in taste? Spicy or bland or rich? How do certain foods make you feel? Comfort foods are called that for a reason. Chicken soup can relieve cold symptoms even as it conjures feelings of well-being, nourishment, and being cared for.

What do you like to see each day? Mountains, lake, ocean, cityscape? Each has a different feeling associated with it. Is nature – flowers, birds, wildlife – important to you? Sight can also stir negative feelings when you observe something you find ugly or distasteful.

Touching something as soft and warm as a lover's hand can stir sensations in your body and give you a sense of security and love. Patting a dog, cat, or other animal can bring a feeling of connection. Touching something sharp can bring a sense of danger or wariness.

When one sense is inactive, your other senses become more acute. All senses are navigation tools. Life is energy and vibration and each sense exposes feelings in your body, your emotions, and your spirit.

Senses and emotions are your life force. How you feel gives you information in every moment. Do you pay attention to those feelings? They can shift at a moment's notice. You have the ability to shift from hate to like to love and from love to like to hate. Living fully is being aware of your feelings and shifting from hate to love, from shame to pride, guilt to goodness, unforgiveness to forgiveness, fear to courage. Life is short. What are you waiting for?

While you are alive is the time to shift perspectives and make amends. What do you want to carry with you into the afterlife? Personally, I want as little as possible. I want the freedom to float, with nothing weighing me down.

Your Contribution to the World

All of this noticing, sensing, and feeling is important as you connect and support those you love through their transitions. As you become more aware, through your senses and emotions, you are better able to listen fully, to be present with your dying one unconditionally, and to have meaningful conversations about your loved one's desires and wishes, without judgment or arguments. You've embraced your shifts toward feeling better, which may then be the guiding light for them to shift. By becoming curious instead of afraid, you can better plan with them how to showcase their life.

Human beings seem to be the only species who question why we are here on this planet right now. We have evolved into intellectual beings... or have we? Sometimes I feel we are human *doings* instead of human *beings*, because we often seem to be more interested in what we are doing than who we are being.

Take a moment and observe yourself. Are you a human doing or a human being? What are you doing? Who are you being? Are you doing what brings you joy and fulfillment? Are you being someone you would be proud to call your friend? If the answer is yes, good for you. I believe this is what living fully is all about. That's your reason for living here and now. If the answer is no, why aren't you? What hurdle are you allowing to be a barrier? What are you choosing not to face? What are you holding onto so tightly that struggle and tug-of-war happens? What would your life look like if you let go – really breathed – felt your life happening in exactly the way you want it to.

Doing what you enjoy and being the best you can be – that is what living fully is about. No regrets. No "I should." No "why didn't I?" No "I wish I had."

What Do You Want Your Family to Know?

Take the time to see where your life is at this moment. Are there things you regret? Make a list of them and then list three reasons why you have that regret. For each reason, list one thing you can do now to change that regret into an accomplishment.

Are there things you feel like you should do? List three things you feel like you should do and then, for each, list one thing you can do to shift "I should" to "I can" or "I will." Do the same for "Why didn't I?" and "I wish I had," listing ways to shift them into positives and choices, to "I did" and "I have done" or "I will do this by" and state a date.

How do you feel now, knowing you can live without regrets and that nasty "should"? What will you do in the future to live without regrets and shoulds?

I encourage you to find the positives, the accomplishments, and the joy in your successes and make a concerted effort to live without the regrets and shoulds. As you accomplish each of those tasks, the possibilities and opportunities for change will appear.

As you do this for yourself, you can also do this with your loved one.

Imagine the gift and the easing of burdens you can give to your loved one by creating this letting-go-of-what-wasn't and focusing-on-what-is exercise with them. Your loved one may not be able to do this as formally, yet the conversations you can have together can relieve some of the emotional distress you both may be feeling.

This is also the opportunity for forgiveness and gratitude to be explored. Where there was struggle, disassociation, hatred, there may now be ease, communication, and love. This process may take time, so take on this challenge sooner than later. You may say, "Oh, I can't. They did this or that to me." I get it. Why punish them or yourself? Why hold onto that grudge? Are you feeling satisfied and justified in your noncommittal to someone? Do you like who you've become? These repressed feelings may be holding you back in life.

We all carry some trauma that defines us and how we live in this world. Trauma is our opportunity to see the larger picture and give forgiveness and have love and compassion. Only then, can a forgiving, compassionate, loving world be created. I do not want to pack resentment, unforgiveness, and hate in my bag as I transition from this world. Do you? Perhaps the less baggage we have, the better.

Before you can support or assist someone else on their journey of forgiveness, compassion, and love, your hurdles need to be at least examined, and preferably jumped over rather than merely gone around. What are you holding onto so tightly you can't let go? As you move through those feelings, you may feel more compassion for yourself and your loved one. *Their* feelings may not change; however, your reaction to them will.

Perhaps, you've not experienced trauma and just know you will be sad and can't imagine not having this person in your life anymore. Instead of focusing on what you won't have, maybe shift and focus on what you have had and still will have.

You can create a celebration of your loved one's life through a legacy project. Often, this type of celebration of life brings much healing to family members and can alleviate some of the sadness and grief.

Exercise: Creating a Legacy Project

If possible, have your loved who is nearing death or faced with an illness co-create this legacy with their family and friends. If that's not possible, family members can create this for them and then share it. Everyone involved would find many benefits in creating this project while the loved one is living. This creation allows for those left behind to have something tangible and positive as a reminder of the contribution their loved one has made while physically here on this planet.

Here are some topics you can speak with your loved one about, or discuss with those who know them: What obstacles have you overcome? What lessons have you learned? Name one thing no one or not many people know about you. Name three things you want your family to know about you. Think of the impact you have made on yourself and family. Where is your happy place?

I had the opportunity to witness the difference in conversations family members had once a legacy project had been created. Not knowing what to say or how to converse with their aging parent, uncomfortable silences, and rehashings of what had been changed into, "Gee, I did not realize you had done that." Or, "I'd forgotten about how much fun we had on our family vacation." Laughter and the sharing of those fun times replaced the woes of the past that could not be changed.

Sharing your thoughts, stories, and lessons learned encourages other family members to do the same. It is also a reminder of your loved one's accomplishments, which really is about celebrating life.

You may want to create, purchase, and/or decorate a special scrapbook containing pictures of places you've traveled to with your loved one and put captions under them. You could include important poems and quotes having special meanings to your loved one. You could make a book of your loved one's favorite recipes and the occasions on which they made them, and relate how the meals made you all feel.

You could suggest your loved one write love letters to each member of their family and their friends, and even to those not born yet, to say what your loved one's hopes and dreams are for each of them.

Perhaps you could create a scroll, decorated and written as a proclamation of your loved one's life. Or, the legacy project could be a video with a personal message for each family member and/or your loved one telling their favorite stories. This could be your loved one's life in review – the positives and also the lessons of the negatives, if your loved one chooses to include them.

The importance of creating this legacy is for your loved one's family and friends to have something tangible when your loved one is gone, and to give your loved one an opportunity to share their memories, thoughts, and poems during their last months, weeks, and days, when no one is quite sure what to say. It can be a wonderful way of connecting.

Sharing your loved one's stories may conjure memories they have had with you and enable them to be fully present, communicating love and joy.

Two resources to help you get started are www.treasuredpassages.com and legacyproject.org's Life Interview Kit.

Make this project enjoyable, creative, and meaningful, as it is a wonderful reflection of your loved one's life. This could be more delightful if created with friends and family members, all sharing their experiences, maybe a reflection of what your loved one has meant to each of them. This will be inspiring and uplifting.

We all have something to contribute to this world, no matter what, and this is truly a fantastic way to showcase ourselves humbly and with grace.

Imagine a son, daughter, cousins you haven't spoken to or seen for a while. Conversations can be difficult when gathering around a loved one who is dying...

and then you show them your celebration project, or your loved one's legacy project. What had been a strained relationship may turn into one of ease and laughter. People, in general, enjoy hearing stories of accomplishments and meaning, especially with so much negativity in the world currently. Here is the chance for you and your loved one to shine your light and give insight into your lives where people might have assumed something different. A true connection can be made, which ultimately may ease pain for all involved as your loved one passes. You've conquered your dragons, made peace with the past, are fully living in the present, and are more peaceful about the future.

I had the good fortune of experiencing a legacy project being created by generations of family members. It was wonderful to witness the sharing between the family and then the joyful conversations and laughter when sharing those experiences with the person dying. That altered the feeling of despair and being somber to a sense of connection, love, and being in the moment. Music and singing filled the room.

Memories created that way are the ones we carry with us in our hearts, regardless of what the past may have been, because we choose to celebrate life and accomplishments. This is a fabulous, loving way for us to exit this physical existence.

Another bonus is you can use this celebration or legacy project at the wake or funeral (if you choose to have one). No one will need to scramble to put some pictures together at the last minute.

Produce this legacy project while you and your loved one are feeling good. Do it with fun, joy, and creativity. Take the time you have to do this, whenever you can, for yourself and for and with your loved one, while they are able and before they die.

This celebration of life can still be done after a loved one has died. Remembering your loved one's contributions to the world may be the ideal way to honor and pay tribute to them and may ease some of the sadness and grief you are feeling. In coming years, you can review the project, to celebrate the anniversary of their birth and death, for example, to look back at the project you all created and reminisce with compassion and love.

Legacy Project Format Options

SCRAPBOOK

Purchase a decorative, meaningful scrapbook to contain pictures and notes and/or decorate one.

- Get a shoebox or file box and separate photographs into sections; for example: family, trips, occasions.

It can be helpful to include the dates.

- Group similar photos together and make captions for those groups, such as where your loved one was and the names of the people they were with.
- Write out a funny story to include with the photos, where appropriate.
- Upon its completion, you may want to include a current photo of your loved one holding the legacy project. And you can take spontaneous photos during the process, as you create it.

SCROLL

- List life accomplishments as proclamations (past).
- List current things your loved one is proud of (present).
- List your loved one's future thoughts and dreams for their family, friends, and the world (future).
- Depending on the size of the lists, obtain a large sheet of parchment or some other durable paper and write each list out clearly, leaving plenty of space between each past, present, and future heading.
- Decorate the sides of the scroll with paint or colored pencils to make it more personal.
- Attach wooden dowels to the top and bottom and tie the ends with colored cord to have it look official.
- Roll the scroll and tie with a colored cord.

VIDEO

- Prepare a script. What does your loved one want you to know about their life? It could be highlights of their childhood years, teen years, high school, college, family life. You can include vacations, favorite places visited, places they did not go but wish they had. Your loved one could describe their favorite car, house, job, experience. What thoughts and wishes do they have for future generations? List all of the people your loved one would like to have included in the video. Have your loved one's family and friends add something about them in the video.

- Find a picturesque, comfortable setting and make the video. You may need to record it in multiple sittings, depending on length of material and what your loved one is capable of.

- Convert the video to DVD for easier viewing. Make sure to share it with your loved one so they can enjoy what has been created.

LETTERS

- List the people your loved one would like to write a letter to.

- You can make audio recordings of what your loved one is saying, so you can then write the letters, if your loved one is no longer able to write. Or you can share the letters in the audio format.

- Letters can be for people who have passed, those living now, and those yet unborn.
- Suggest your loved one include what they would like each person to know about your loved one and what your loved one's dream is for each.

RECIPE BOOK OR BOX

- Inquire as to your loved one's favorite meals; either those they prepared or those that were prepared for them by someone else. List the occasion. Collect the recipes and ask if there are any additions or changes to be made to them. Catalog and type these recipes, or print them on file cards, and create file boxes for them. You could duplicate them for family members to have.
- Decorate the recipe box or book.

NOTES

CHAPTER 3

Transition Room

---

*"Every moment that you spend in the
conscious awareness of God's Presence
becomes another building block on the
super-structure of your house not made with
hands – your secret dwelling place in the
magical wonderland of My Kingdom.
Here in this mystical sanctuary, you will find
the peace that transcends all human
knowledge and understanding… here you
will find your abode of harmony, abundance,
spiritual wholeness, and eternal rapture."*

—Don Mardak

A transition room is the place your loved one will spend their last month, week, day or moments before they pass on. The thought of your loved one passing certainly can be sad and upsetting. By creating a sacred space for them and you; joy, peace, and serenity can be established during this difficult time.

We decorate each room in our homes and embrace their loveliness. We also have choices as to how we want our transition room to be. This is our sacred space.

First, consider where your loved one wants to be during this time. Do they prefer their (almost) final resting place to be at home, in a care facility, or in the hospital?

These are some of the vital questions to ask your loved one while they are still able to respond.

Atmosphere

This is your opportunity to create your loved one's space exactly the way they want it. Perhaps your loved one enjoys gazing out the window. Soft lighting can emit a sense of calm and peacefulness. Or your loved one might consider bright lights more comforting. Special photos and pictures surrounding them would allow your loved one to conjure great memories and remind them of fond times shared with favorite people.

The aroma of lavender permeating the room may elicit a feeling of calmness, peacefulness, and serenity. Or you could use rose or another scent your loved one finds pleasing. Placing your loved one's favorite flowers around the room brings a refreshing scent as well as joy to your loved one and to those who visit. Scented candles could be used, giving off a complementary fragrance.

You may not think these things matter; however, the more comfortable you can help your loved one feel in their space and with their body, the less pain and struggle they may have as they transition. The texture of their pajamas, sheets, and blankets are important to ease possible agitation, as are the pillows. Perhaps your loved one has special pillows they especially enjoy. The sensation of touch is a way to connect, and allowing that connection to be as your loved one likes can bring them feelings of comfort, caring, and love.

Our sense of hearing is our most acute, thus the last sense to leave our body. Even people who are deaf can tap into the vibrational energy of sound. Comforting sounds could include a cascading water feature, songs from places traveled, or peaceful instrumental, meditative, angelic music. Or there could be simple, soft background music. Have your loved one make several musical selections.

As your loved one's breathing changes during this stage of life, tapping into the cadence of someone's voice or the beat of music can relieve anxiety and pain by giving their mind something else to focus on. This may also bring calm, peace, and serenity to you or someone else sitting in the room with your loved one.

You and your loved one set the stage for creating this sacred space. Having your loved one state their wishes alleviates the guesswork for the family. This also allows those visiting to come in to your loved one's unique place of tranquility with respect, ease, and peace.

If a care facility or hospital is preferred as a transition room, there may not be as many choices. When your loved one makes their wishes known, however, many facilities can be accommodating.

Decide if your loved one wants to have machines sustaining their life, or if they choose to not have the beeps and noise. Some selections your loved one may have the option to consider in a facility are: private or shared room, being near a window to look out, what they wear, blankets, possibly pillows, lighting, candles, aromas, flowers, pictures, books, poetry, music, people who visit.

Even though your loved one is in a public facility, a sacred space can still be created for them, especially when their wishes are stated. This also allows the family, friends visiting to relax and communicate. While your loved one is lying seemingly unconscious, friendly family voices and music will still be heard and may relieve anxiety.

Sitting Vigil

You may also consider having someone sit with your loved one around the clock. This is referred to as *sitting vigil* and is usually done in shifts.

Companionship for your loved one at this time – knowing they are physically not alone – can relieve your loved one's anxiety and give them a sense of comfort and love. Knowing someone is present with your loved one, can help you rest. Most hospitals and care facilities do not provide this service, and you can retain the services of an end of life doula, or seek out the local hospice agency, as many of them do provide vigil service.

I have witnessed the peacefulness someone feels when another person is fully present with them at the time of transition. There can be pain, anxiety, and struggle to breathe, especially at the end. Having someone hold their hand, speak soothingly and lovingly to them, which they can hear, releases their mind from angst and allows their body to relax and ease into its dying process. I have witnessed the adjustment in breathing when a person is touched and spoken to. It appears the struggle to breathe eases, and even the tenseness of the body relaxes and returns to a natural rhythm, and then finally ceases in calmness. I don't know what is actually happening in the body; however, I can sense the serenity and peace of having someone present who cares.

Listening to music and softly communicating with your loved one changes the energy of the room. Nurses have commented when coming into an ICU unit where machines were beeping, how peaceful the room was because of soft music and the telling of a story. The nurses didn't want to leave the feeling of comfort present in the room.

I can't stress enough how helpful it can be to create this sacred atmosphere for yourself and your loved one while you and they are able. This can make all the difference between a death of struggle and pain, and one of peace, serenity, and ease. Being in a loud room with the television blaring, bright lights beaming down on your loved one, who's barely covered, may be the last thing your loved one truly wants as they transition – and the last thing you want to remember. Being, instead, in a private, quiet setting with low lights and little noise may give your loved one and you the peace you both seek.

We die, either way. I prefer the peaceful transition. We exit the world much the way we come into the world. We can expand and be unrestrained or we can stay constricted out of fear. The baby will be born, either way, and we will die, either way. Which is the preference of your loved one? Which do you prefer?

Prayer

This poem taped to the outside of the sacred room can be a reminder to all those entering the room to come in fully present.

I ask you humbly to be present with me here

in this moment – this instant in time.

I ask you to breathe – slowly, deeply, completely –

from the tips of your toes to the end of each hair strand.

I ask you to feel your breath move through you and

allow it to relax and center you.

Just for a moment...

Just for this moment...

I ask you...

Be present with me and breathe.

–Anonymous

Here are some useful facts. Once the body expires (and, by the way, the body knows how to die), stops breathing, you can stay with your loved one and pray, create a ceremony, and just be. Decomposition of the body does not take place for many hours. If your loved one is at a hospital or care facility, let them know when the breathing has stopped, so they can proclaim the time of death necessary for the death certificate. Then you can stay as long as you like, uninterrupted.

If your loved one dies at home, you can call a nurse to come and proclaim the time of death. This does not need to happen right away either. Someone can make a note of the time of death and that is the time the nurse will use. Again, there is no need to do anything with the body right away. Sitting with the body in its non-breathing state can be quite comforting. There is an unexplainable energy surrounding the still, warm, flexible body, which creates a peacefulness. You can also witness all the struggle of life is gone, and only serenity and calm exist.

Some rituals for the dead include bathing the body, washing hands and feet, changing the clothes, and just remembering the wonderful times spent with your loved one.

The body can be preserved for up to three days using dry ice. Even for an open casket ceremony, there is no need for invasive toxic embalming. Caskets can be rented or, if time allows, you can have family and friends build a casket while other family members make the lining for the inside. These caskets can then be decorated. This is another way of honoring your loved one.

The movie *In The Parlor: The Final Goodbye* is a home death care film. It's worth seeing, even if you and your loved one choose not to have a home death, as it contains valuable information about death and dying and may give you and your loved one further insight into how peaceful the dying process can be.

Exercise: Transition Room Questions

Where does your loved one prefer to be?

- In the middle of life happening around them?
- In a private, yet close-by bedroom?
- Away from all the hubbub in a quiet setting?

What does your loved one want their room to look like?

- Windows open? Curtains open or drawn back?
- Candlelight? An eternal flame glowing? Nightlights?
- Will there be icons (crosses, angel figures)?
- Which flowers? Would the flowers have a scent?

What sheets, pillows, and blankets would be most comforting?

- A soft mattress? Or one that's more firm? One with heat pads?
- Does your loved one want to be dressed in comfy soft flannel pajamas or something more formal?

How does your loved one want their room to smell?

- With lavender aromatherapy permeating the room?
- Scented candles to enhance the flower's scent?
- Room spray?

What sounds does your loved one find most soothing?

- The cascading of water from a fountain? Nature sounds, like ocean waves, rainforest, or perhaps something other?
- What type of music does your loved one enjoy? Do certain genres of music positively alter your loved one's mood or recall pleasing memories?
- What poems or books would your loved one appreciate having read to them?

How would your loved one like to be touched?

- Have their hands held?
- Be given light massages, using lotion or oil, rubbing their arms, legs, or feet?

- What else do they prefer?
- When people enter your loved one's room, would your loved one prefer to have one person visit at a time or come in as a group?
- Is there a flavor your loved one enjoys more than others – for their lip balm, for instance.

Remind your loved one all of these decisions are flexible and may be altered as they wish, and even at a moment's notice.

NOTES

CHAPTER 4

Visualizations

"There is a beach where the sound of the sea speaks peace. Where the infinite sky remembers and every grain of sand welcomes the feet, the paws, the claws, the life that press upon them. That's where I join the tides and the sun."

—Sally Mackinnon

I understand the sorrow and grief you may feel at the thought of losing a loved one. I have found the more you can communicate with your loved one and prepare for their death, the more your loved one's transition – and yours in letting them go – will occur in a more supportive, loving, gentle way.

Visualizations are a great tool for relieving the pain and anxiety around dying, as this imagery can provide comfort and ease – through recalling a favorite place visited, for example – thus taking your loved one's mind off the pain they may be feeling.

The ability to have inner vision enables the brain/mind to focus on something other than what is right in front of us. Reading, or listening to certain excerpts, allows our imagination to conjure up images. These mental illustrations are pleasing and can elicit a relaxed, calm response in our system. Much is the same when we share a visualization with someone who is in pain, distress, or is anxious. Hearing the cadence of a familiar voice depicting scenes from a favorite place can calm the breath, disperse the pain, and bring ease as the mind focuses on the images you've evoked instead of the pain.

Reason

The following story illustrates the power of imagination:

Two elderly men shared the same room at a healthcare facility. One man, able to sit up for an hour each day, could gaze out the window. His roommate was on the other side of the room, by the door, and not mobile enough to sit up.

The men spent their days together chatting about their lives, where they grew up, childhood escapades, jobs they'd had, and their homes, wives, children, and dreams.

Each day as the man by the window sat up, he would describe what he saw outside.

"The mountains are glowing today. Some of the trees' leaves have changed from green to a vibrant yellow as the sun shines upon them. Next to the yellow leaves are bright red leaves, as red as a male cardinal's feathers, and mixed with those leaves are brilliant orange ones, creating a kaleidoscope of color, glittering as the wind gently ruffles them. Each tree seems to enhance the beauty of the trees next to it, while the turquoise blue of the sky is the backdrop. Below, children are raking fallen leaves and jumping into them with delight while they are throwing leaves into the air. Other people are strolling, arm in arm, through the park, stopping to admire this beautiful warm afternoon. Ducks are wading and swimming in the lake, which reflects the glorious colors of the sky, clouds, and trees. Swan boats are gliding by, carrying spectators who are enjoying their last rides of the season."

Oh how the man in the bed by the door looked forward to this one hour every day. The view out the window must be fabulous, and it seemed to change quite frequently.

One day, the man by the window described the activities of people enjoying a concert. Even though they couldn't hear the music, it seemed from the description like everyone was having a most fabulous time. They were dancing, laughing, and singing

– young and old alike. They were eating cotton candy and taking turns riding on a multi-colored animal carousel. As the man by the window described the scene, the other man vividly imagined the delight and frivolity of all the people having fun, dressed in their festive clothing.

One day, a nurse came in to find the man by the window had died peacefully in his sleep. A while later, the man by the door asked if he could be moved next to the window, so he could view all he had envisioned. After he was moved and had finally managed to lift himself up enough to look out the window, he was amazed to find a solid view of the building across the alley. He rang for the nurse and asked how long the building had been there. Her reply was the building had been there since before the hospital was built. When the man told the nurse the story of the daily descriptions of the world beyond the window, she smiled and said, "Ah, your roommate was blind and couldn't see the building."

As the man lay back down, he remembered the visions he had been given all of those days, and felt immense gratitude for his roommate, who had been so generous with his descriptions.

The Power of Imagination

You can create personalized visualizations with your loved one.

As their transition nears, their eyes are usually closed. Imagine the peace and ease for your loved one upon being able to visualize the beauty they've actually experienced. These visualizations can actually change the struggle of breathing to the ease of breath. These created images can often relieve pain, and you can actually observe the body relax its tension into calmness. By sharing visualizations, you've given your loved one's mind something else to focus on.

Background music can be a nice addition to the visualization. Also, having the visualization pre-recorded can be beneficial if someone needs to step away from your loved one's room for a while. You can record visualizations in your voice, a family member's voice, or your loved one's voice. You may choose to create a few different visualizations.

This exercise allows for more communication and sharing about places your loved one has traveled to. The more detailed, specific, and descriptive you can be, the better.

Have your loved one describe a scene as if sharing it with a blind person who is there beside them. Have them use all five senses to complete the picture – what do they hear, smell, see, taste, and how does this place make them feel? The feeling of the place elicits the most comfort.

Reading and sharing these visualizations may also transport you to a different place and time, thus bringing a sense of calm and serenity to you, too.

Visualizations are a type of meditation. They change the breathing pattern and body tenseness. I find them useful when I'm feeling stressed, or when my mind has too much chatter. Being transported to another place and time changes how I feel and brings me to a state of greater peacefulness and remembrance. May you and your loved one's visualizations give you the same feeling. There is tremendous satisfaction in making others happy, despite our own personal problems. Shared grief is half the sorrow, and happiness when shared, is doubled.

Exercise: Creation, Meditation, Visualization

Try this exercise to create your loved one's personal visualization. Even if they've never meditated, they can ease into this. Background music may be helpful to increase a relaxed state of mind.

Have your loved one sit in a comfortable chair, or lie down with their eyes closed, if possible. And ask them the following questions (you can print these questions out so you can easily write down the answers, or you can record the answers to transcribe later):

- Where is your favorite place in nature?
- Are there animals there? What type of animals? What are the animals doing? What types of noises are they making?
- What types of flowers are there? What colors of flowers and what do they smell like? What types of trees are there? What season is it? Is the wind blowing?
- Are you walking, sitting, swimming, or flying in this place? If walking, are you barefoot? What does the ground beneath you feel like? Is it soft, wet, dry? How do you feel while walking? If sitting, are you on a blanket or chair or something else? Describe it in detail. If you are swimming, where are you? Are you floating? What's the temperature of the water? How does the water make you feel? What color is the water? (Even if you happen to know their answers before they say them, the more detail they can give you the better, as this will help when organizing and recalling the visualization for them). If flying, are there clouds? Are you in an airplane, hot air balloon, kite, hang

glider? Are you gliding? Is the sun shining? What is the quality of the air? How does this experience make you feel?

- What aromas surround you? What do these scents remind you of?
- What do you hear? Are leaves moving? Are birds chirping? Is music being played? Are there voices? Whose voices?
- Is there a flavor this place brings to mind? Are you eating anything? If so, is it sweet or spicy or something else? How does eating this make you feel?

Once all these questions are answered, you are ready to create your loved one's visualization.

Here is an example of a visualization I created and I use for myself. I love how it makes me feel when I transport myself to this place. Reading this to your loved one might be a way to begin exploring visualizations with them.

The warm, white, soft sand beneath my feet and between my toes gives me the sense of being grounded in the earth. As I gaze at the turquoise water, the warm rays of the sun embrace me in a comforting hug, filling me with serenity. The gentle breeze rustling the fronds of the palm trees keeps me cool, calm, and refreshed. I put down my orange, pink, and blue striped blanket and pink chair in the perfect spot of seclusion under a low branch offering me soothing shade. Before I sit down, I leisurely stroll around, making a path in the deep, soft sand down to the crystal-clear, azure water, and splash my toes in the water. I can see the bottom of pure white sand as a few brave yellow and blue fish dart about.

Oh, I love this warm, refreshing water as it now laps against my ankles, beckoning me to go in deeper and deeper, which I do, until I find myself immersed in this tranquil sea. I stretch out, so magnificently buoyant that I can easily float on the surface without much effort. The sound of the water gently slapping against me fills me with wonderment and peacefulness. Floating on this wondrous ocean, I sense what may be similar to the feeling of floating on a puffy, white cloud. I have no care in the world, no pain, no struggle – just beauty and ecstasy. Above and around me, pelicans soar just above the turquoise water, searching for their favorite fish for dinner. Dolphins are making their way over to me, easily, casually, swimming and sometimes jumping as they enjoy this most perfect, relaxing day. And I continue to float without a care in the world.

As I roll to my stomach, I observe the zebra-striped fish in their glory of blues, yellows, reds, and oranges, darting to and fro.

Now I venture back to the warmth of the sand and sit in my chair on my blanket in the unfiltered sun and allow the gentle breezes to caress my body, drying me ever so carefully. I sip on a cooling, yummy, strawberry piña colada while I sit in my comfy, padded, bright pink chair, observing happy children splashing in the water and enjoying this splendid day, as well.

This is just one example of what you can create. Your loved one might prefer a mountain scene, a cabin on a lake, or another possibility. Wherever your loved one decides, is perfect for their visualization.

You can use my visualization to inspire you to have fun generating one with your loved one. It is a great way to get really descriptive, and you may decide to use a familiar place to you both and expand it to bring it more to life. Or it can be a place of fantasy.

Mostly, you want your loved one to be able to relate and experience a remembered place again, as if for the first time. If it's a fantasy place, you have unlimited freedom to create something they enjoy. Have at least two visualizations if possible. As you read the visualization, you can add more adjectives to paint a more descriptive picture.

Many times, as we wander through life, we tend to forget to see the small details. I've found, after creating these visualizations, I pay more attention to life happening around me, see more colors and variations, notice cloud formations, notice how a bird flies – flapping its wings a lot or gliding on the thermals. Does it have any unusual markings? And that butterfly, what type of flower attracts it and what type of butterfly is it? I notice more noises around me – some pleasant, some invasive – and more scents (is it time to take out the garbage?). You may find your awareness heightened and your loved one may, as well. A gift in itself is observing and participating in life happening all around you both.

Some visualizations may elicit messages from your loved one. I find those to be ones where the listener is not relating to a familiar place, yet they are transported there and can visualize what you describe and may want to comment on it afterward.

It's important during this phase of transition to give the mind the least amount of work to do and, instead, distract it from what may be happening to your loved one's body. The mind may think the body is in pain when, in fact, the body is adjusting to a slowing down and is engaging in its natural process of death. Dying need not be painful or a struggle.

Creating and sharing visualizations with your loved one may give you a sense of accomplishment, knowing you can ease their pain and – if the visualization is based on a shared memory – embark on a familiar journey with them. These visualization images can replace some of the sadness with the remembered joy of pleasant times spent together in peace.

"Draw your focus and senses to this moment, here resides the expanse of energetic communications. The music of your interconnected, consensus expression sings within the frequency of your cells. Pay attention to how you feel."

–Edel O'Mahony

NOTES

CHAPTER 5

Rituals

"We are not alone. The spirits of those gone before guide our steps, our traditions, our beliefs. We are not alone. The care of those around us leads us to healing and wholeness and comfort. We are not alone."

—Mohawk/Onondaga Healer

A ritual is a ceremony or action performed in a customary way, in sacred, customary ways of celebrating as a religion or culture. Rituals are acts regularly repeated in a set, precise manner.

Establishing rituals with someone while they are still alive is a great way to honor them. It gives them something to look forward to each time they see you.

Why Use Rituals?

Taking the time to sit and just be with your loved one may be the greatest present you can give them.

Not only are you giving them your time and attention, you are giving them your love, unconditionally.

As we age or become ill, time becomes more precious, and so making some part of the day or a visit special may bring a burst of happiness and appreciation to your loved one, and thus to you.

One ritual could include having tea together. Great, inspired conversations may happen during this time. Stories may be shared, or maybe an experience of bonded silence and heartfelt connection.

Another ritual may be to take a walk together in nature, if your loved one is able. They may be reluctant at first, yet, with a little encouragement, movement and a change of scenery can elicit a change of perspective and this gives you both something to do. Conversation about neighbors and flowers may be instigated.

Another ritual may be meditating together or listening to your loved one's favorite music.

Another option would be to take a ride together to somewhere you both enjoy, where there will be few distractions. It may be to a nice garden, a park with benches, a beach, or a favorite restaurant – somewhere you can go to be together fully and is a special place you would want to visit together regularly – once a week, or whenever, you set the time and frequency.

Witnessing a loved one suffer is extremely difficult and may have you feeling helpless. Sharing your love unconditionally with your loved one may ease their pain and suffering. Love is the universal language and is something we all desire. You may not understand the power of love, yet giving and receiving love makes a huge difference. Creating your ritual together includes the element of sharing love.

Often, having a ritual gives your loved one something to look forward to, either during your visit or during the day. Having something constant your loved one can count on can be very reassuring to them during this often uneasy stage of life.

Rituals help build pleasant memories of times spent together, fully being present with one another. As time goes on, and especially if you become the primary caregiver, take at least half an hour a day just to be present with your loved one, without distractions. Too often, chores and daily living get in the way of just being together.

When I was younger, I visited my grandmother at her home. She always had homemade snickerdoodle cookies and we would make root beer floats. As time progressed and she was no longer able to make the cookies and floats, I would take them to her. Oh, the laughs and fun we had! For those couple of hours, we traveled back in time, reminiscing about those lazy afternoons we'd shared. She would often remark on how grateful she was I remembered our favorite times together. My gram always made me feel special and, in turn, I was able to do the same for her, honoring her. It has been many, many years since her transition, and yet, taking time to create this ritual with her is a memory that lives in my heart, along with many others.

Develop a ritual suited best for you and your loved one. What a gift you'll be giving them! You can share memories of special times spent together, while sharing the love you have for them.

You can use the ritual in the creation of their visualization.

In the end, having that cup of tea or walk in nature or meditation may bring you the peace and comfort you are seeking, replacing some of the sorrow you may be feeling.

You can create rituals after your loved one has passed, centered around their birthday, your birthday, a wedding anniversary, and/or their transition day. You could acquire a special plant to be added to your garden in their memory. Sometimes, having flowers of your loved one's favorite variety in your home can bring a smile and elicit fond memories. Perhaps sitting and sipping freshly brewed tea or your loved one's favorite beverage, and toasting your loved one on their auspicious occasion will help. Sure, the memories may be painful, so reminisce on the happy, fun-filled, laughter-inducing times. Try to remember your loved one's smiling face and the joy you felt together. Let that visual replace your loved one's end of life demeanor. Conjuring up those wonderful memories may replace those of the less great ones, and leave you with a smile on your face and warmth in your heart. After all, your loved one would want you to remember the special times you shared together.

What will your special ritual or routine be – with your transitioning loved one, and after they have passed? Will every anniversary occasion have a different routine? Will they include a variety of people?

Another way to honor your loved one is to provide a special book in your loved one's name to your local library. You can make a donation to your loved one's favorite charity, or take food to a local food pantry. In creating something positive around your loved one's special day, you are recognizing their contribution to the world in a loving, thoughtful, and honoring way.

Creating rituals eases sadness and replaces sorrow with a pleasant memory of your loved one. May this bring light into your heart and assist you in living in this present moment.

Whatever you decide the ritual to be, if a donation of some kind is appropriate, consider including it in the obituary (an obituary is a written celebration confirming your loved one's life and death).

Exercise: Creating a Ritual

- What time of day will your ritual with your loved one take place?
- What type of beverage does your loved one like?
- Purchase or use a special mug, china cup, or glass just for this time you are spending together.
- Use special plates for snacks coordinating with the cup/mug/glass, to be used just for this time together.
- Decide how long you would like your ritual together to last.
- Light a special candle at the beginning of your time together and, when the ritual is complete, blow the candle out. This creates a beginning, middle, and end of your special ritual time together.
- Set the intention to be fully present with each other and to keep the conversations cheerful, easy, and fun. Maybe reminisce about vacations taken together.

NOTES

CHAPTER 6
Writing the Obituary

"If you feel something calling you to dance or write or paint or sing, please refuse to worry about whether you are good enough. Just do it. Be generous. Offer a gift to the world no one else can offer: YOURSELF"

—Glennon Doyle Melton

The legacy project was about creating a keepsake of your loved one's life. Assisting your loved one with writing their own obituary is another way of honoring them. First, imagine writing your own obituary. This will help you relate to your loved one during the process.

A Life in Review

What would you want people to know about you if you were transitioning now? Formulating your obituary first may make it easier for you to create this with your loved one, as you can use yourself as an example and use your obituary as a template. Creating this with your loved one gives them the opportunity to share what is and has been important in their life in a concise manner.

Much like the legacy project, this is a celebration of who they are. Instead of thinking this is morbid, consider it opening the door of reflection as a way to honor your loved one's life. I understand this may be a very difficult concept to think about, especially while you and your loved one may be healthy. I feel your potential sadness as you consider having to prepare this with and for your loved one. Just think, though, you will not have to write this after your loved one has passed and you are caught up in all your emotions, perhaps excluding some important information they would have wanted included.

Here are some questions to consider while writing the obituary. You may also want to read some other obituaries to get a clearer vision of how you and your loved one want to be represented.

- Name (married and maiden)
- Date of birth
- Where resides; where spent most of life living
- Education

- People honoring the passing: usually husband/wife, siblings, children and their spouses, grandchildren, great grandchildren, nieces/nephews
- List of accomplishments: what are they (or you) most proud their life represented.
- Where the service, if any, will be held
- Where donations are to be sent
- Online guest book information

I fully understand the sensitivity needed in creating this. Again, writing your own obituary – also not easy – may be beneficial in creating one with your loved one.

Even though this conversation may seem morbid, it truly is another way of sharing and honoring your loved one, especially if it's done in a kind, fact-finding way. This also may open the door for conversation about their wishes for their memorial service or celebration.

Considering a Service

I have found that even non-religious people tend to want some sort of service. We are humans of community, and sharing sorrow, grief, and memories enables us to be open and receiving of the kindness and love others show us at this time. This feeling of community is important during this time of sorrow.

Many cultures observe this ritual of honoring the deceased. This is the opportunity for people to pay tribute to your loved one and celebrate their life, as well as pay respects to you and your family. Even if a relationship is strained, this celebration may ease some of the angst and negative feelings, creating space for forgiveness (it's never too late) and true, unconditional love to shine through. A service can be a beautiful example of love, understanding, and grace for all in attendance to witness.

So, what do you and your loved one want your celebration of them to be like, look like, and feel like? As you gain clarity and honesty around what you desire, you open the conversation with your loved one through the expression of your wishes. This may then, in turn, give your loved one the permission and ease to think about and discuss their desires in a gently fun-loving way.

Many times, the reason our loved ones don't like to share their death thoughts with us is because they feel it will be too upsetting for us. Part of this is them feeling they are leaving us behind. Having these discussions can create the opportunity for you to let your loved one know, you will be okay (of course, only say that if you mean it). You can let them know you will certainly miss them, and you are prepared to move on with your life. This knowing usually gives your loved one a very reassured feeling and peace of mind. It also gives them the permission to let go and pass – in many cases more easily, feeling you will be okay and taken care of. Just as you do not wish to witness your loved one struggle, your loved one does not wish to leave you in struggle either.

Exercise: Questions to Ponder

If your loved one has not attended church on a regular basis, is there someone you or your loved one knows who could perform the ceremony, if you choose to have one? Other questions may arise, like these:

- Where will this ceremony/celebration take place? In a church, synagogue, funeral home, someone's home, or out in nature?
- Is the music at the service different from the music in their transition room? Is it inspirational, uplifting? Will it be played on a CD player or will a choir or group be singing? Do you need to hire a pianist, organist, or guitarist?
- What types of flowers most represent your loved one?
- Will there be a specific reading? A eulogy? What will the reading be and who will give it? Who will give the eulogy?

- Will a formal mass be included?
- Will you give a slide presentation of favorite memories?
- Where will your loved one's celebration occur? Does your loved one want to be present during the service – meaning will their casket be present?
- Will you be having a viewing of the body beforehand?
- Will there be a gathering after the service? If so, will it be at the church, at someone's home, at a restaurant?
- Will there be a burial at a cemetery? Which people will attend? Will it be private, with close family only?
- Will someone be speaking at the burial?
- Will you place flowers, shovel dirt on the grave, or will your loved one be cremated? Will you spread ashes in different places? If so, who would attend? Will you share the ashes with various people?
- Will there be a military service at the gravesite, will a flag be presented?

You may want to allow some extra time in the service for people to share their stories about your loved one.

These questions may not be easy to discuss, and the planning of a service for a loved one who has passed is often dreaded or does not occur at all. However, it is important to have these planning conversations, because they help us process our feelings and our grief.

We plan for weddings, vacations, and other special occasions, often leaving our death plans until the very last minute. Instead of being carefully and thoughtfully planned, those ceremonies are usually rushed and we are in a scramble to put all the pieces together. Sure, the scrambling might ease or numb some of the pain, grief, and sorrow briefly, only to have them return tenfold after all the festivities are over.

Think about how much more rested and relaxed you will be if all this planning is done ahead of time. Putting this plan in place allows for a true tribute and honoring of your loved one the way your *loved one* would wish it to be, without excluding anything.

There are various pieces to the creation of the love/death plan puzzle to consider now, not only for your loved one, but also for you and your family members. Imagine the gift of having all this taken care of. Then there's no guesswork or wondering what your loved one's wishes were.

As you come to terms with death, conversations surrounding death change. Fear has subsided for you and you are thus able to dispel some of the fear for your loved one. The unknown has become more tangible and only the *mystery* of life and death continues.

The more we all can speak about death, about our fears and concerns, the more we can be at ease about death and speak nonchalantly about our inevitable end of life.

During the process of creating a celebration plan, you may realize death is not final. We are, in fact, eternal. Your loved one's physical life on Earth may have ceased; however, (I believe) our spirit and our soul live on eternally.

Staying open and curious to the wonder of life and death may assist you in having a continued connection with your loved one. Part of life is noticing life happening around you. In the death of someone tender, dear, and meaningful to you, staying present, aware, and conscious may allow you to notice your loved one in a butterfly, in the eyes of a baby, in the loving lick from a pet, in the gentle caress of a friend, or in a beautifully colorful rainbow.

Our loved ones continue to impact our lives, even when they have physically gone.

Live your best life, and remember the joy, love, connection you shared together. Your beliefs may be different than mine. Feel into what your beliefs are. Feel what is true for you and what gives you solace, comfort, peace, and joy when thinking of and remembering your loved one.

NOTES

CHAPTER 7

Wishes

"One of the greatest blessings pain and loss offers us is their remarkable ability to put everything in perspective, and remind us of what is truly important."

—Barbara DeAngelis

We all have the ability to make choices in life. We also have the ability to make choices about how we want our death to be.

Where to Die

We spoke in a previous chapter about what your loved one's room would look like, feel like, smell like, and sound like. Now that we've explored the possibly difficult tasks of writing the obituary and deciding things about the service, let's back up and consider where this transition room will be. Then we can look more specifically at other aspects of the transition you and you loved one may wish to review.

Where does your loved one want to die? Please rest assured, whichever place your loved one is considering, where they choose is the ideal place for them. Often times, your loved one may not even be aware there is a choice. Whatever your loved one's choice is, the support and love you give them at this time can be your most wonderful expression of love. How you present yourself and your support makes a difference to your loved one's ease and peacefulness. If you are disproving of their choice, your loved one may become worried and want to comfort you and change their mind, instead of being where they need to be for *their* transition.

So, let's look at the home choice. There are many benefits to having a loved one die in their own home or one of a family member. You and your loved one can create the atmosphere exactly the way you want it. Activity and a sense of belonging as living is occurring all around your loved one has them enjoying being a part of life instead of being isolated or in an unfamiliar place. This can be a way of honoring your loved one, their decision, and their transition. Being at home also creates a sense of security and allows family members and friends to come and visit at times most convenient for you and your loved one. Pain and discomfort can be more easily managed, and your loved one's care and needs more readily met.

Of course, at this time, it may be helpful to consult with an end of life doula, a nurse from a medical hospice, someone from a volunteer hospice, or a visiting nurse. Such people are familiar with home deaths and you can consult with them about pain management, if that is required. They may also give you guidelines as to what to expect during this dying process and what to look for as the end nears. End of life doulas have been trained to recognize certain signs, know what medications may be useful (although they typically do not dispense them), and suggest how to properly care for your loved one (for example, sometimes moistened swabs can keep the lips from drying too much and becoming cracked). Doulas have also been trained in how to sit vigil (sitting vigil can also occur at a facility). Being with someone at the end of their life is an honor and a privilege.

Being with Death

Witnessing the body do its job of dying is as miraculous as watching the birth of a baby. The body just *knows*. Most people I have spoken to about being present as a person expires conclude the experience is very peaceful, tranquil, and beautiful, which is not what we may automatically think.

Death is not morbid. Death is a transition from this life into the next, creating the Mystery. Sitting vigil with your loved one means being with them completely. No agenda, expectation, or thoughts about how bored you may be, just be with them fully and holding space, with tenderness and love, with them and for them. Even though their eyes may be closed and their breathing shallow, your loved one knows, feels, and senses your presence of unconditional love and compassion.

For this reason alone, be very clear about how *you* feel during this tender time of sitting vigil. Grief and sorrow are part of life, as is sadness. You don't necessarily have to put on a brave face for your loved one. However, the more you can be with them as they are right now, the more serene and peaceful their passing will be. It may be helpful to remember your loved one is concerned for your well-being, even at the very end.

Sometimes, people in transition hold on longer than necessary because they are afraid to let go and leave the ones they love. Letting your loved one know, although you will miss them, you will be okay, can be very helpful to them. Remind them you have support from family and friends. You may want to share a future vacation or travel plan. Your loved one, knowing you are taken care of, will be more able to let go and release the struggle of trying to stay alive.

What's also very helpful is providing the permission for your loved one to let go. Saying something like, "I am here with you now and I understand this is your time to go. I love you and I release you to the mystery of death." Hearing those words, or something similar, (remember, sound is the last sense to leave the body) allows your loved one to relax and let go, knowing all is well with you.

I have seen that, at some point toward the end, there is an excitement, which may be noticed in the fluttering of the eyes or unusual quickness of breath. This seems to be an intuitive understanding your loved one has, knowing they are not alone, guardian angels, loved ones gone before them, are welcoming your loved one home to them. Feel into how this resonates with you. Can you accept this as a possibility? If yes, why? If no, why not? Try to understand and just be with your loved one and support their beliefs, even if you do not agree. This acceptance of beliefs is also a mystery of death.

Until we experience death ourselves, which we all will, we don't really know for sure what happens. Be really honest with where you are in any death talk with your loved one. The more open you are, the more open your loved one may be encouraged to be.

Self-Care

Continually check in with yourself to see how you are feeling – emotionally, spiritually, and physically. Where in your body are you holding tension?

Self-care is very important, during this time especially. Take the time to have a massage, go for a walk in nature, meet with friends. Be honest about how you are feeling. You may want to seek counseling. You are important during all of this planning and during your loved one's transition. The more you take care of yourself, the better you are able to assist your loved one and your family.

Dying in Place

If a home death is chosen, when you and your family are ready, you contact a medical person, like a nurse, to come to declare the time of death. Sit with your now-deceased loved one, just be with them. You can hold them, talk to them. Many people have remarked at how the spirit/soul of a person stays in the room (even if the death occurs at a facility) for many hours after the breath and heart have stopped. Observe how peaceful your loved one is. No more pain. No more distress. No more struggle. There can even be a childlike quality to their face. To me, this is what being fully alive and living is – witnessing the tranquility of death. Doing so may ease some of the fear you've had surrounding death. After all, your loved one has just become your teacher, showing you how not to be afraid. That is a true gift, in and of itself, for you and your family members, as it may change your experience and feelings about death.

You may decide to create a ritual or ceremony (see the previous chapter) for your loved one at this time. This is another opportunity to honor your loved one and yourself for sharing this unique experience together. You may choose to wash your loved one and dress them in a farewell outfit.

If a hospital facility is chosen as the place you and your loved one decide to be at the end, there are some thoughts to ponder. Medical personnel – doctors and nurses – are trained to keep people alive. Be very clear about what your loved one's wishes are during this time. Be very precise about what you and your loved one want to have happen. Does your loved one want to receive oxygen? A morphine drip? Have a ventilator? Do they want to be turned? Bathed? Have their lips moistened or have water nearby to drink? These options may prolong the dying process. Allowing the body to simply be and to do its job can, often times, be the best medicine.

Ask yourself, are you doing things for the comfort of your loved one or for your own ease? Be very clear of your intentions. I cannot stress this enough.

If the transition is taking place at a hospital, ask the hospital facility if they have private rooms or areas that are quieter than others, and what their protocol is for caring for your loved one. Knowing the answers to your questions beforehand may alter where your loved one wants to spend their last days, or may give them more comfort, because then your loved one knows what to expect.

Depending on the privacy and location of the room, you may be able to create a special atmosphere, as discussed previously, providing music, reading material, photographs, and flowers to create a serene, sacred setting in an otherwise sterile space.

Be very thorough about what you and your loved one's needs and expectations are. If possible, you may want to visit the hospital beforehand.

A health care facility may give you a little more flexibility than a hospital. Typically, they have more awareness around end-of-life transitions and may not be as committed to keeping someone unnecessarily alive when it is their time to go. It is still important, however, to check the facility's protocol around the care of a dying patient. There are belief systems in place around when oxygen, morphine, or a ventilator may give the patient more comfort, even as they pass. However, the use of visualizations, being in a relaxed, serene atmosphere, and having loved ones present are equally important and necessary.

Remember about self-care through all of these decisions. You may want to check in with yourself to see how you are feeling. It may be helpful to discuss your thoughts with friends, a counselor, an end of life doula or your family. Knowing you are truly not alone with all *your* feelings may bring you the comfort and ease you need to facilitate this end of life transition for your loved one.

The clearer you can be in your understanding and fear of death, the more transparent you can be in having these discussions with your loved one. Fear is an emotion we can alter by having the courage to have "the death discussion," in an open and frank way.

Being prepared is the key to a more peaceful transition. Be proactive instead of reactive. You may have time to be prepared, if either old age or a drawn-out illness has occurred; or you may not, if something sudden has happened. Either way, being as prepared as you are able to be takes the guesswork out of the process and keeps you from getting lost in thinking, "Oh, crap.

Now what?"

You may feel the more you can include your loved one in living until the last breath and heartbeat, the more you are living fully with them. Regardless of where your loved one decides to transition, you can lie with them in bed and hold them lovingly. Being close provides comfort, security, and love to both you and your loved one.

Casket, Cremation, and Burial Choices

You and your loved one have the final resting place decided, so now it's time for what happens next. Here are some thoughts to consider as you and your loved one look at and make choices you may not have been aware of. Your discussion could even begin with, "Did you know you have choices about what will happen to you after you have passed?"

If you choose a casket, what you may not realize is that you can rent caskets for the wake or funeral, if you and your loved one choose to have one. Many funeral homes won't tell you that is an option, but it is. Renting a casket allows your loved one to be present during the service, but then cremated, for example. You may want to research to find a funeral home having this option, which often may reduce the funeral expenses.

Also, your loved one is not required to be embalmed, even with an open casket. Dry ice will preserve the body beautifully for up to three days. The military often uses this form of preservation when sending fallen soldiers home. Unfortunately, some funeral homes have a policy stating a body must be embalmed. This is a falsehood, and you may want to seek a funeral home more compliant with your wishes. Embalming can be an invasive and demeaning way to preserve your loved one's body, and those toxic chemicals are put into the earth or released into the air.

There is also the option of having your loved one's casket made, decorated, and lined by family members and friends. The materials used could be biodegradable, which is better for our environment. Willow caskets are an option, providing a complete, biodegradable burial.

Did you know there is also a green burial choice? This option includes being buried without being embalmed, in a pure wood casket without metal fasteners of any kind, and then buried in the ground without a cement vault or cement covering. Willow caskets are also used for this. Traditional cemeteries are extremely toxic, take up valuable land space and put unnatural elements into the earth that never fully decompose. First there are the embalming chemicals, then a metal or elaborate wood (mahogany or teak) casket loaded with metal, copper, or gold accoutrements, and then the cement vault, plus the pesticides and herbicides used to reduce insect and weed infiltration.

These can be difficult discussions; however, in this day and age of awareness and environmental protection, consider how you or your loved one want to be remembered or buried. Any choice you make is the ideal choice for you both. Just be aware there are options.

Currently, only a handful of states allow green burials. However, you can transport your loved one to one of the states offering this option. A way of honoring of your loved one is to leave no toxic print on this earth. Embalming is incredibly invasive to the body, and no state has a mandate for it (unless the body is toxically diseased). A pure wood casket, including wood nails and fasteners, can be put in the ground without a vault. A green burial decision requires a bit more maintenance from the cemetery, as they must continue to refill the soil as the body and container decompose. Also, there is no use of pesticides or herbicides. This is a true way of the body returning naturally to the earth.

Another way of honoring your loved one's life may be the donation of organs to support the life of someone still living. This is a legacy in and of itself. The site liveonny.org is a source for organ donations. You can also make preplanning arrangements for the whole-body donation of your loved one. Often, there is no cost to the family for a whole body donation. After the body has provided all the information needed for research, the ashes are returned to the family. This plan must be arranged for before death, through lifelegacy.org.

Many diseases can be researched from a donated body, thus creating a lasting legacy and assistance for finding cures. These cadavers are also used for training in the medical field.

These issues may be another, "Did you know...?" conversation-starter to educate your loved one of choices available and to find out what their wishes are.

As difficult as these discussions can be, imagine the education, understanding, and knowledgeable decision you and your loved one will be able to make. You may want to research these options more fully before presenting them to your loved one. Be clear, first, as to what your choice would be, and keep an open mind and heart as you listen to your loved one's choices. Staying in a place of acceptance and love can bring this often difficult discussion into one of ease and create a stance of curiosity.

Continue to assess how all of this information is making *you* feel. Take the time to honor yourself during this love and death plan. Have a massage, go for a walk, speak with friends, seek counseling, and/ or discuss all these options with an End of Life Doula.

Education and preparation with your loved one will continue to create some stability and peace surrounding what's happening, and promote courage instead of fear for you both.

Some resources to explore are (and you'll find more at the end of the book): funerals.org and gbc.org, both of which are non-profit organizations showcasing alternative possibilities to traditional funerals. Other sites to consider are fcaslo.org, homefuneralalliance. org, thresholds.us. You may want to view the movie *In the Parlor: The Final Goodbye*, which is a documentary about home funerals.

Exercise: Taking Care of Yourself

Check in with yourself about your feelings around where your loved one wants to die. You can use your body as a compass to find your way and to tune in to how you are feeling and where you are holding tension.

Are you feeling sad, anxious, depressed? Where are you holding those emotions in your body?

What is one thing you can do to right now to relieve any uncomfortable feeling you are having to some degree? What about taking a few deep breaths, going for a walk, having a cup of tea, calling a friend?

Did that help? Are you feeling some relief? What is one thing you can do to honor yourself to recognize and further sink into whatever you may be feeling during this time.

NOTES

CHAPTER 8

Logistics

"As I have struggled with the mystery of my death, seeking the meaning of this life, I have found what I am looking for. It is very simple. We are here to learn. Everything that happens to us helps our learning. And nothing helps us learn more than death."

—M. Scott Peck, MD

Another issue to explore to help with being prepared for your loved one's transition is the decision of whether or not to accept medical assistance during a crisis, an emergency, and/or at end of life.

Medical Directives

There are legal documents you can obtain from your loved one's physician or hospital that deal with what your loved one wishes to have happen during different medical situations. "DNR – Do Not Resuscitate means to withhold cardiopulmonary resuscitation (CPR) or advanced cardiac life support (ACLS) in respect of the wishes of a patient in case their heart were to stop or they were to stop breathing" (Wikipedia). Another legal form is the POLST – Physician Order for Life-Sustaining Treatment. These forms can be found at polst.org.

This decision may be difficult (as if any of the other ones have been easy!) initially, yet having these documents in place may save your loved one from traumatic "rescue" treatments, causing possible further illness and suffering. This is a way to address the issue of *quality* of life versus *quantity* of life.

The fact is, your loved one is going to die, maybe even sooner than you or they expect, and so this is where tough love and tough answers are needed. Will the quality of your loved one's life be improved by having life-saving measures taken, or are you just prolonging the inevitable?

Without a directive in place, the medical staff, if called on, will do whatever is necessary to keep someone alive, even if it is not in the best interest of you and your loved one, which is why being prepared is so important.

A great resource to assist you in beginning these difficult conversations is codaalliance.org. This organization has Go Wish Cards you, your loved one, and your family members may find to be valuable as conversation starters.

Another resource is Five Wishes. "Five Wishes is America's most popular living will because it's written in every day language and helps people express their wishes in areas that matter most, the personal and spiritual in addition to the medical and legal. It also helps describe what good care means to you, whether you are seriously ill or not. It allows your caregiver to know exactly what you want" (excerpted from the book *The Last Visit*, by Margaret Dodson). More information can be found at thelastvisit.com.

Once you have gathered information and presented it to your loved one, an attorney specializing in health directives may be your next call, though completing these forms with the assistance of an attorney is not required.

Support your loved one through this process. The more information concisely written down, the better the chance for follow-through and a peaceful serene transition. Being prepared and completing all forms early on ensures your loved one's rights are being protected. This will give you peace of mind, knowing your loved one's wishes are being followed, especially during a time of crisis or emergency, when so much is happening around you and emotions may be at an all-time high or low. After all, seeing a loved one suffer may be one of the most difficult challenges we face as humans.

The next tough challenge may be letting your loved one go. Keeping your loved one alive so you have more time with them may not be in your loved one's best interest.

As you go through this process with your loved one and give them support, be clear about what your needs are and what your loved one's death will mean to you. A great resource for this is caringinfo.org.

Once this medical directive is complete, you post it on your loved one's refrigerator, so it is more likely to be seen if emergency medical aid needs to be called. Also, keep a copy in your loved one's purse or wallet, and your own, in case they are transported to the hospital without you. EMTs will look for this directive before they begin any type of life-saving initiatives. If a directive is not found, the EMTs will have no idea what the preferred protocol is, especially in the case of an emergency, and may perform life-saving measures when your loved one didn't really want that.

Will and Trust

When all the heavy lifting of the medical aspects of documentation has taken place, you may choose to have the discussion with your loved one about a will. This may not be any easier of a topic to discuss, yet is also necessary. Often, if wishes are put in writing before the loved one passes, much possible discourse can be avoided with the family afterward.

Naming an executor of the will and letting family members know who that is may increase family harmony doing this difficult time of grief and sorrow. Also helpful can be retaining the services of an attorney you and your loved one trust to ensure all of your loved one's wishes are being thoughtfully carried out. An attorney is trained to ask specific questions and may be able to pose the questions a certain way to get all the necessary answers from your loved one.

Remember to include the end of life plan, the burial, and ceremony choices as you discuss these arrangements. I have seen the more dialogue families have regarding these decisions, the more peaceful and harmonious the passing of the loved one is, as worry about family fighting has often been relieved. After all, this is about supporting your loved one and each other during this transitional phase of life. Whatever is helpful to support each other more easily is worth the effort.

An end of life doula, and/or a funeral concierge can be contacted to advocate and assist you and your loved one during this decision-making process. Being prepared with information and wishes clearly stated before a crisis occurs can ease the burden you all may feel at this emotional time.

Exercise: Stating Wishes

What decisions would you make for your own end of life, and why? Pondering these questions yourself can give you clarity as to what is important, thus opening the door for discussion with your loved one.

Here are some specific questions to ask your loved one:

- Who is someone you would like to be your health proxy, to provide information to the medical staff if you are not able?
- Do you want to be resuscitated if you stop breathing? Right away, or after a few minutes?
- What life-saving measures are to be taken to keep you alive? Being hooked up to a ventilator to provide breathing? Having a feeding tube inserted to keep you alive? Having morphine drip to keep you medicated?
- Would you be willing to post your copy of the medical directive on your refrigerator and carry a copy with you?

- What are the possessions you would like to leave to special individuals? (Then you can help to label and document them.)
- Who would you like the guardian or executor of your will and trust to be?
- Who is your estate (house, money, etc.) to be left to?
- Would you like to write a letter to any family members, or to the family in general, to let them know of your wishes while you are sound of mind?

NOTES

CHAPTER 9

Communication with Loved Ones on the Other Side

"We are not alone. The spirits of those gone before guide our steps, our traditions, our beliefs. We are not alone. The care of those around us leads us to healing and wholeness and comfort. We are not alone."

—Mohawk/Onodaga Healer

Communication with our loved ones after they pass is possible. There are many mediums – people who can communicate with those on the other side, who have a way to connect those of us physically here with those who have passed from this dimension.

How do you feel about this realization?

Do you feel more comforted knowing your loved one has not totally "died" and may be living in a different dimension and realm? Does the premise you can communicate with them ease your burden or grief?

As your mind and heart remains open, you may hear or notice your loved one signaling to you. A bird you never noticed or is not regularly in your region may become more prominent and chirp incessantly, trying to get your attention. A stray cat or dog may wander onto your doorstep looking for a new home. You may notice coins on the ground, feathers along your path, or a heart shaped rock in front of you. Your favorite song or a song familiar to the two of you may come on the radio the exact moment you are thinking of your loved one.

Are these coincidences? I think not. I believe they are true signs our loved ones are around us and want us to know of their presence.

Beyond the Veil

Communication with our loved ones after they have departed this earthly realm has enabled many people to find peace and solace, from realizing there is more to death than the disintegration of a body. The soul and spirit live on.

This has also been documented in several books regarding people who have "died," only to be brought back to life to share their experience of "dying." These experiences are helpful in our understanding and our relationship to the mystery of death. Reading about the experiences people have had may help alleviate some of the grief and sadness you may be feeling, helping you know your loved one does live on in another realm. *Dying to Be Me*, by Anita Moorjani, *Proof of Heaven*, by Dr. Eben Alexander, and *Proof of Angels*, by Ptolemy Tompkins and Tyler Beddoes are books on this topic you may be interested in reading.

Sure, you are no longer able to touch or hold your loved one, or carry on two-way conversations, and yet, knowing your loved one is around you, guiding you, may relieve some of the distress you may be feeling.

Once your loved one passes, they are no longer burdened by their incapacities, whether of an illness or old age. Your loved one is whole, unencumbered by any ailments. This is another reason to celebrate the way you most remember them, instead of the way your loved one looked at the time of passing, if that was difficult for you. Imagine your loved one reunited with their loved ones who have passed, even including a favorite pet.

I believe our loved ones encourage us to explore the possibility of something *other* at the end of life.

There are many experienced mediums ready to assist you with this understanding of *something* after death and continued communication and guidance with your loved ones. Would you find solace in communicating with your loved one? What would you want your loved one to know about your life since they passed? Would your loved one want you to feel sad or to have joy in your life? What would bring you joy at this time?

The Possibility of Afterlife

As a medium, I understand the feelings/intuition/ voices I hear that encourage me to contact a relative living on this earthly plane.

One day, as I was meditating, a voice clearly asked me to contact his mother. I faintly knew of this person and his mother, just as acquaintances, people I'd rarely seen, yet did say hello to. I had no idea how to contact his mother, other than through a mutual friend. I heard his voice at the beginning of February. Unfortunately, the mother was out of state and would not returning until the middle of March. Communication would have to wait until then.

The mom, Helen, was very open and excited to be hearing from her son, Greg. Helen and I chatted for a bit and then Greg spiritually came into the room. He wanted his mom to know he was whole and complete and thought of her often. This was the first communication they'd had since his death two years prior. He encouraged her to continue moving on with her life and not to be so sad anymore. He wanted her to know he missed her, his dad, and his sister, and knew they missed him also.

I then mentioned to Helen that Greg really wanted to be in touch with her in the beginning of February, on February 4th, to be exact. She said, "Oh, that's my birthday." Helen, after the shock wore off and tears subsided, smiled and said to me, "Thank you for this message. Greg always made me feel special on my birthday, either bringing me hand-picked flowers or candy." As she continued to speak about her son, a glow of light glistened on her face where shadows had previously been. Helen had been given the gift of knowing her son was okay and she could communicate with him often. A part of him lived on again in her heart. This was a true healing and a loving experience to witness.

For me to be able to bring those two loving people together is truly a gift, and one I never take for granted. Being open to knowing anything and everything is possible and probable allows me to keep my channels open for communication and for much healing to occur. If this type of communication interests you, seek out a medium who has this ability so you may also have continued connection with your loved one.

So, what are *your* thoughts about the afterlife? What would you like to believe about afterlife? What are you afraid of believing? What would you say or ask your loved one who's on the other side?

There are many theories to explore and much to discover, so search out the theory that resonates the most with you. Perhaps this means attending a meeting or a workshop where a medium will be communicating with loved ones and providing proof of an afterlife. An option is to attend a medium's session with your loved one before your loved one passes, so they may understand what is possible in the afterlife, thus lessening fears your loved one may have surrounding death. What better gift than to have your loved one communicate with their loved ones who have passed on and gain some insight into what is possible and what they may expect after they pass. By sharing this experience with your loved one, they and you may realize they are truly not alone and will truly not be alone throughout this challenging part of life.

The loved ones who have passed before you want you to know you are not alone. Some people reincarnate, some become guides, while others become angels. All beings are here to assist you with your life.

Your life definitely will change after a loved one dies – there is no question about that. However, keeping an open mind and heart to the mystery and possibilities of life after death may be consoling for you. Many Eastern and Native American cultures believe the soul and spirit live on, which is why they have created such elaborate ceremonies surrounding the deaths of loved ones. They send their loved ones off into the next realm in the most loving, cherished ways. How beautiful. Imagine honoring your loved one the same way. You can give your loved one a send-off as if they were taking an extended vacation, which is exactly what your loved one may be doing. This realization can be very enlightening for you and your family.

There are several mediums who have evidence of life after death. Two of my teachers, Robert Brown and John Edward, have books you may want to take a look at (see the References section at the end of this book).

Be open in heart and mind and you, too, may feel the embrace of your loved one who has passed on.

"I cherish who I am becoming.
Loss requires a new way of living."

–Unknown

Exercise: Signs your Loved One Is Near You

You can decide how you would like to be shown your loved one is around you. For example:

- Finding a rock in the shape of a heart.
- Finding a meaningful shell.
- Coins appearing on the ground.
- Feathers appearing on your path – maybe certain types, like white, or black.
- Your favorite song playing on the radio while you think of your loved one, or their favorite song plays on their birthday or the anniversary of their death.
- A wandering pet comes into your life.

Daily or weekly, recite a familiar prayer your loved one enjoyed. Listen for any messages or intuitions you may receive from them.

Light a candle and write in your journal without any forethought or expectation. Let the pen ink flow freely on the page. When you feel complete with the writing, read over what has been written. Notice the feelings you have in your body. You can also pose a concern or question you have and then write and let your pen flow across the page. Then read what has been written to see what insights have come to you.

You can recreate the ritual you had with your loved one during their time of transition, noticing any intuitions you may receive as you do. Awareness of your feelings is important during this time of transition. Honor yourself by creating a new ritual in your day.

CHAPTER 10

Enhancements

"If we could see the miracle of a single flower clearly, our whole life would change."

—Jack Kornfield

The use of essential oils and crystals during your loved one's transition time can be beneficial for you both. These elements of nature can promote a sense of well-being, peacefulness, and serenity. Essential oil scents can be relaxing and the energy of the crystals can assist the body to rest in ease and calm, and may relieve pain.

Essential Oils

Nature provides us with all we need. Essential oils derived from plants and crystals formed from the core of the earth may assist you and your loved one during the difficult discussion process and then during the transition time. You may find them useful also for your life and your well-being in general.

The use of essential oils can aid in relaxation, providing more calmness and peacefulness. Using essential oils can ease pain and distress and can comfort the mind as well as the body.

When preparing to have an important discussion, you can infuse tea or a glass of water with lemon essential oil and/or peppermint essential oil. Maybe have a lavender essential oil diffuser scenting the air in the background. These particular essential oils promote a feeling of well-being and bring a sense of calm. These are appropriate to use for any type of stress you or your loved one may be feeling, at any time, not just around these "end of life" conversations or during your loved one's transition time.

There are also a wide variety of essential oils used for specific ailments. Native Americans and Eastern cultures used essential oils long before it was introduced into our modern society.

"Essential oils are more than just highly concentrated plant extracts. Most possess potent medicinal qualities, and many are valued for their exceptional cosmetic qualities. While the whole plants or plant parts they are derived from possess beneficial qualities, essential oils are much more powerful" (excerpted from the book *Essential Oils for Beginners*, by Althea Press, which is a great resource; www.altheapress.com).

Many people find aromatherapy useful for bringing a sense of spiritual well-being. Frankincense is an example of an essential oil used for centuries to add fragrance and serenity to sacred spaces such as churches, sanctuaries, and home meditation rooms. This may be a wonderful oil to add to your loved one's room during their transition. Diffusing frankincense and taking long slow breaths can help you and your loved one focus as they embark on their spiritual journey.

Essential oils have fantastic positive effects on every level, enhancing mind, body, and spirit. Aromatherapy is the creative use of essential oils to evoke positive changes on aesthetic and mystical levels, as well.

Become familiar with essential oils if you are not already. Relieving stress and restoring balance are important for your self-care. Lavender, bergamot, juniper, and patchouli essential oils combined together can do that nicely.

Here are a couple of tinctures you may want to make for you and your loved one, to promote tranquility.

BALANCING LAVENDER AROMATHERAPY BLEND

When tension needs taming, this balancing lavender aromatherapy blend calms and refreshes. Juniper, bergamot, and patchouli essential oils promote peaceful feelings, while lavender has a slight sedative effect that helps to take the edge off.

- 14 drops bergamot essential oil
- 14 drops lavender essential oil
- 2 drops juniper essential oil
- 2 drops patchouli essential oil

Combine the essential oils and diffuse or blend with distilled water for use as a room spray. This also is a great blend for a bath or to use on a washcloth when bathing. Add 4 drops of this essential mixture to bathwater and relax.

REFRESHING VANILLA-ROSE BODY SPRAY

Enjoy a sense of calm that lasts all day with this delightful antibacterial body spray. Not only do rose otto and lavender essential oils prevent body odor, they promote a sense of calm, and the vanilla helps enhance mood and bring on a feeling of total well-being.

- 12 drops rose otto essential oil
- 3 drops lavender essential oil
- 1 drop vanilla essential oil
- 1 ounce distilled water

Combine all the oils, then mix them with the distilled water in a small spray bottle. Spritz the blend onto bare skin after showering or bathing or after gently washing the skin. This is also a great mixture to rub onto your loved one's skin when bathing is no longer wanted, as they may find this mixture soothing.

Crystals

The use of crystals can also be helpful in relieving pain and stress. Crystals have been used for millennia to heal and bring balance. They work through resonance and vibration.

You can find benefits in using crystals for relief from common ailments. Amethyst is known for its calming, healing properties. Rose quartz opens the heart to receive and give more love.

Placing crystals around your loved one may bring more peace and soothing than certain medications might. You can carry a crystal with you, one that resonates with you, for balance and a sense of security. Most crystal stores have educated and knowledgeable staff who can assist you in finding the ideal crystal for you and for your loved one. Going to a crystal store together might be a nice outing for you both and may generate spontaneous conversations about what crystals you both are drawn to and would want to have around you. One resource I use is *The Crystal Bible; A Definitive Guide To Crystals*, by Judy Hall. This reference book has pictures of the stones, gems, crystals as well as descriptions and the crystal's healing properties.

The more comfort you can provide yourself and your loved one using natural resources, the less stressful this transition time may be. Bringing nature into your loved one's room especially with the intention of well-being, serenity and peace boosts the body to do its job as the body naturally resonates with these types of elements. And you may find the qualities of the essential oils and crystals resonating with *your* peace and ease and well-being also.

* * *

Life is a journey we all embark on from the day we are born. Thankfully, we have choices as to what this journey/adventure/life may look like. By living fully, authentically, passionately, you can then expire resting assured you lived with only a few regrets maybe. You loved, gave forgiveness, understanding, and compassion, and allowed all those you came into contact with the ability to do the same. By living well, your loved one can die well. I believe these four sentences are necessary for living fully: *I forgive you. Please forgive me. Thank you. I love you.*

Here's to you, and to both life and death.

"Life's journey is not to arrive at the grave safely in a well preserved body, but to skid in sideways, totally worn out, Shouting, "HOLY SHIT"......
What A Ride!"

–Ya!

NOTES

Conclusion

Consider the idea, neither your loved one nor you have to wait until after death to celebrate your life the way you want to.

Earlier this year, James Burrows, the famous TV sitcom director for the shows *Taxi, Cheers, Frasier, Will and Grace, Friends*, and *The Big Bang Theory* was honored for directing his 1,000th episode. During his speech, he commented on how wonderful it was to be honored with this tribute while he was alive. "I would have hated missing this," he said.

Although your loved one may not be as famous as James Burrows, having a celebration honoring your loved one's life while they are alive can be a rewarding, meaningful, and loving experience. If you wait until your loved one dies to celebrate, then the celebration is for everyone except your loved one. So why wait?

When David Bowie knew he was dying, he put together a special album honoring his life and music. That was his tribute to himself, showcasing his life. Glenn Frey, on the other hand, relied on his band members to memorialize him after he died, and that has not happened yet.

Creating a legacy with your loved one while they are alive showcases their life in review and allows you both to share in the celebration of life here and now. Every life has positive attributes to remember and realizing your loved one's life worth, from their perspective, and no matter how trivial it may seem, can be gratifying.

* * *

Give "death" feelings a chance to express themselves. What does death mean to you? Are you afraid of death? Why? The more you explore your feelings surrounding death, the more you may find yourself living differently. As you become clearer about your choices surrounding death, the easier you may be able to have death conversations with your loved one.

Education and preparation for your end of life and that of a loved one enables you both to live fully and peacefully, knowing all has been taken care of. You and your loved one have the opportunity to make conscious, well-thought-out decisions about what your loved one's end of life will look like, feel like, smell like, sound like, and where they want to be cared for during their transition. The more your loved one's choices are discussed and documented, the greater their chance of having their wishes fulfilled and the ease of their transition.

Life has a conclusion; however, it may not be the end. We are like flowers, starting as a seed that's planted, watered, and nourished, strengthening so it can then push itself up from its dark home under the soil. The stem then grows leaves and has a bud that blossoms into its full glory and splendor, to then die and become nourishment for the next seed. Its form has changed, yet its life continues through to the next flower. Perhaps we do the same. We begin as a seed, receive water and nourishment, come to be born, live in our glory, and then expire, returning to the mystery of death, leaving space for something other to be born in ourselves and the ones we leave behind.

Your death story begins with you. Like anything in your life, your story is written by you. Before you can have a conversation about the end of life with someone you love, you may want to have the conversation with someone else you love – yourself.

Imagine feeling into what is possible for you to create at the end of life as you have been creating in the now of life. Knowing your feelings, dealing with them, sharing them, may give you a sense of empowerment, and may also encourage your loved ones to explore their true feelings about life and death. Imagine our lives not really being over when we die; rather, just beginning in some other realm.

You have the tools to explore and discover what may lay ahead. You are in control, just as your loved one can be. The more curiosity, discovery, and knowledge you bring to the process, the more voice and preparation you have. Imagine the difference you can make in your own life, your loved one's life, and your family's lives. Death becomes no longer a morbid topic to be avoided. Death becomes a topic to be openly discussed, embraced, and given time and care to.

Every conclusion breeds a birth into something other. As this book comes to its conclusion, my hope and dream is you will birth your courage for peeking into the subject of death.

Don't only cry because someone has died, and in doing so left you; smile because they shared their life with you. No matter how short or long their life was, joy and fun has been shared. How fortunate you are!

Goodbyes are not always easy. It is how you handle the goodbyes that make the difference. You have the choice to say goodbye knowing you have held your loved one in the most loving, compassionate way, or to leave with regrets. You have the choice, so consider saying goodbye lovingly, compassionately, and gracefully. You can say, "I'm going to miss you and I love you."

Even though death may be the conclusion, you never know what the next chapter of life will be.

A part of me went with you

A part of you stayed with me

I AM FOREVER CHANGED

Your life continues with me

Your love lives on with me

YOU ARE FOREVER WITH ME

–grief toolbox

Epilogue

I write this final page as an addition to my book as it is in its final editing stage.

My partner and former husband recently died suddenly. Even though we had divorced, the loss is felt deep in my heart. True love never really dies, even in divorce. Love shifts from one aspect of caring to a different aspect of caring while apart. I will celebrate the life and love I've had with this man, who is the father of my children.

My heart has opened to a new dimension of love – the deep, deep love and gratitude we were able to rekindle in our friendship. He will always live in my heart and be my guide through the remainder of my life. He will always be the guiding light in our children's lives and our grandchildren's lives. My heart holds the loving memories of our life together.

No matter who has died in your life, open your heart to embrace and feel them. Celebrate love and allow all else to fade away.

You are here, You are there, You are everywhere.

I hold You in my heart and in my dreams and everywhere in between.

I see You in the sky, in the clouds as they pass by.

I hear You in the song of the bird and remember our silly flirts.

I feel You as the wind gently blows, caressing me wherever I go.

You are here, You are there, You are everywhere.

-Susan B. Mercer

Resources

Books

- James Van Praagh, *Adventures of the Soul* and *Healing Grief*, among others
- Anita Moorjani, *Dying to Be Me*
- Dr. Eben Alexander, *Proof of Heaven*
- John Edward, *Crossing Over and One Last Time*
- Robert Brown, *We Are Eternal*
- Ruth Montgomery, *Here and Hereafter*
- Ptolemy Tompkins and Tyler Beddoes, *Proof of Angels*
- Stephen Jenkinson, *Die Wise*
- Karen M. Wyatt, MD, *What Really Matters*
- Thich Nhat Hanh, *No Death, No Fear*
- Judy Hall, *The Crystal Bible*
- Althea Press, *Essential Oils for Beginners*

Movies

- *The Griefwalker*, Stephen Jenkinson: nfb.ca/film/griefwalker
- *In the Parlor: The Final Goodbye*, a home death-care film: intheparlor.com
- *Lives Well Lived*: lives-well-lived.com

Websites

- treasuredpassages.com
- marsha-kay.com
- legacyproject.org
- liveonny.org
- lifelegacy.org
- funerals.org
- gbc.org
- fcaslo.org
- homefuneralalliance.org
- thresholds.us
- thelastvisit.com
- codaalliance.org
- caring info.org
- polst.org
- mobar.org

About the Author

Susan B. Mercer of Modern Outlooks is an End of Life Doula, Kundalini Reiki Practitioner, Energy Healer, Space Clearer, Intuitive/Medium, Educator, and Interior Designer.

Her ability to connect with individuals and spiritual beings has enabled her to assist many people through their life transitions. Whether she is redesigning a room, transforming a home, coaching someone through life's upheavals, or helping them prepare for their death, Susan takes the time to listen to each person's desires and assists them in making decisions with clarity, thoughtfulness, and love.

Susan's experience sitting vigil with people through their end of life transition has given her insight into what is lacking in death-speak. Unafraid of death herself, Susan offers a compassionate perspective on creating a peaceful serene space, which she believes to be so helpful for the ease of passing. Her philosophy of being prepared and stating wishes alleviates the fear of the unknown for her client and their families.

Susan celebrates life while providing serenity during the dying process.

Acknowledgments

Many people and life/death experiences have assisted me in the creation of this book: Tracy Bigelow-Sturgell, for her hospice training and support throughout this process; Henry Fersko-Weiss of INELDA, for the End of Life Doula training which allowed me to witness death with more compassion and inner guidance; A.M. and J.M., for showing me how a peaceful death can exist because of true love; my son, Jason, and daughter, Jenny, for believing their mom can make a difference in people's lives; Anthony, Rachel and the girls for their support; Kenneth, Emily, Stephen, Ashley, and Nicola Mercer, for encouraging their aunt to get her message out to the world; Doug and Donna, Matthew and Alicia for their support; my parents, Mimi and Ken, who have supported me through this process and who have been willing to speak about death and being prepared; my friends who have supported me along the way, including Christine Wetzel, Debbie Pielech, Donna Lipari, Kathleen MacMahon, Julie Kelly, Cari Leversee, Ashley Gable, Joel and Heidi Roberts, and Ron Holt, and many others.

This book would not have been possible without the leadership of Angela Lauria, without my tribe on this journey, and without Grace Kerina and her unwavering support, encouragement, and editing skills.

I appreciate and am grateful to each of you.

Thank You

Are you wondering how to create a legacy project, which one to do, or how to have the conversation with your loved one before you begin a legacy project? You can find a checklist of questions to ask your loved one on my website. This will assist you both in making the determination about which legacy project is best and then how to implement it.

Also, I will create a personal visualization for you to share with your loved one and for you while you are in this transition phase. I find these to be helpful to ease stress and bring a sense of calm and serenity.

You will find helpful information in the blog articles I have written regarding death.

Check out these and other resources on my website at modernoutlooks.com, or email me at susan@modernoutlooks.com.

difference press

Difference Press offers entrepreneurs, including life coaches, healers, consultants, and community leaders, a comprehensive solution to get their books written, published, and promoted. A boutique-style alternative to self-publishing, Difference Press boasts a fair and easy-to-understand profit structure, low-priced author copies, and author-friendly contract terms. Its founder, Dr. Angela Lauria, has been bringing to life the literary ventures of hundreds of authors-in-transformation since 1994.

LET'S MAKE A DIFFERENCE WITH YOUR BOOK

You've seen other people make a difference with a book. Now it's your turn. If you are ready to stop watching and start taking massive action, reach out.

"Yes, I'm ready!"

In a market where hundreds of thousands books are published every year and are never heard from again, all participants of The Author Incubator have bestsellers that are actively changing lives and making a difference.

"In two years we've created over 250 bestselling books in a row, 90% from first-time authors." We do this by selecting the highest quality and highest potential applicants for our future programs.

Our program doesn't just teach you how to write a book—our team of coaches, developmental editors, copy editors, art directors, and marketing experts incubate you from book idea to published bestseller, ensuring that the book you create can actually make a difference in the world. Then we give you the training you need to use your book to make the difference you want to make in the world, or to create a business out of serving your readers. If you have life-or world-changing ideas or services, a servant's heart, and the willingness to do what it REALLY takes to make a difference in the world with your book, go to http://theauthorincubator.com/apply/ to complete an application for the program today.

Lasting Love At Last: The Gay Guide To Attracting the Relationship of Your Dreams

by Amari Ice

...But I'm Not Racist!: Tools for Well-Meaning Whites

by Kathy Obear

Who the Fuck Am I To Be a Coach: A Warrior's Guide to Building a Wildly Successful Coaching Business From the Inside Out

by Megan Jo Wilson

Your Key to the Akashic Records: Fulfill Your Soul's Highest Potential

by Jiayuh Chyan

Standing Up: From Renegade Professor to Middle-Aged Comic

by Ada Cheng

Finding Time to Lead: Seven Practices to Unleash Outrageous Potential

by Leslie Peters

CPSIA information can be obtained
at www.ICGtesting.com
Printed in the USA
LVOW03s0032030118
561598LV00002B/3/P